Alfalfa

The Story of a Duck from Lake Afton in Yardley, PA

by Michelle Gaudet Sharer

BATTLE GROUND
creative

Preface

I live next to Lake Afton in Yardley, Pennsylvania.
I greatly enjoy watching the ducks, geese, and wildlife that I see at the lake. Each spring, I look forward to seeing a Canadian goose, Mallard duck, or Pekin duck sitting on her nest as she waits for her eggs to hatch. Each egg takes about 28 days to hatch and the mother ducks must sit on their eggs for 23 hours per day in order to properly incubate them.

In the spring of 2012, I unexpectedly became the mother of a Pekin duck, who I named Alfalfa. When I would tell people about him, they would often ask lots of questions. I would then show them pictures of Alfalfa and tell them my story.

Nowadays, when folks see me around town and ask how I'm doing, their next question is typically "How's Alfalfa?" Who would think a duck could be so intriguing? Alfalfa certainly has that effect on people.

This is his story.

Acknowledgements

I would like to offer a special "thank you" to all of
my family and friends who encouraged me to write this
book. I'm especially grateful that my neighbor, Samantha,
interviewed me for her school project, which posed the
question, "Do animals imprint on humans?"

Samantha, you got the wheels turning in my head!
Alfalfa certainly did imprint on me. He is as much
of a family member to me as I am to him.

— Michelle Sharer

The white ducks pictured below are Pekin ducks that made their home on the banks of Lake Afton in the spring of 2012. The female duck is swimming in front of the male duck.

At night, the Pekin ducks slept
on our patio, next to the lake.

Unlike the other ducks, the female duck didn't lay her eggs in a nest.
Instead of making a protective nest for her eggs, she laid her
eggs on our patio.

The first egg we saw disappeared, most likely eaten by an animal.
We decided if she laid any more eggs on our patio, we would attempt to
incubate them and release any ducklings that hatched into the lake.
We researched and read books about incubating duck eggs
and raising ducklings and asked questions at
the local feed mill supply store.

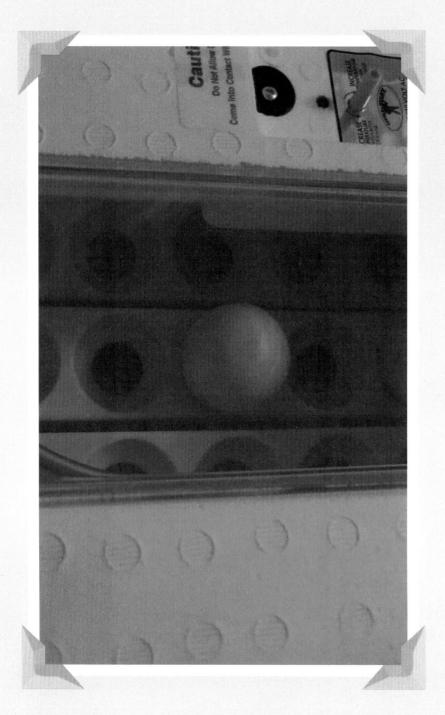

We knew we would need to buy an incubator to keep the egg(s) warm since the mother duck was not present. (We would often refer to the Pekin ducks we would see on the lake as "egg donors.") A mother duck sits on her eggs for 23 hours a day to keep them warm. This allows the baby ducks to grow inside of the eggs for approximately 28 days before they hatch. She turns her eggs every 6 hours using just her bill. I decided to buy an automatic egg turner (pictured left) rather than turning the eggs by hand every 6 hours.

The "egg donors" soon laid two eggs on our patio, which we put in the incubator. We then began counting the days.

After thirty days in the incubator, the first
duck began to break through its shell.
We were excited, wondering what the newly
hatched duckling would look like.

The duck seemed to be taking a
long time to hatch, so I did some research
and learned that a duckling won't come
out of its shell if there is too much light
surrounding the egg.

I realized that it's dark around an egg
when a mother duck is sitting on it.
So, I covered the window of the incubator
with sticky notes. We were amazed to see
our duckling hatch in just a few hours! Alfalfa was born on May 20, 2012.
It was love at first sight.

Alfalfa had to stay inside the incubator
until it was safe to come out, once his feathers
were fluffy and dry. Sadly, the other
egg never hatched.

After we took our duckling out of the
incubator, we placed him in a large tub
with pine shavings lining the bottom so
he would have a nice bed. Baby ducks, like
human babies, sleep a lot and grow while
they are sleeping.

Once our duckling hatched, we used a special heat lamp to keep him warm while he sat in his tub. We used a thermometer to make sure he didn't get too hot or too cold.

Ducklings hatched by a mother duck will follow her around and try to eat what she eats. However, ducklings that are hatched in an incubator are fed chick feed. Our duckling refused to eat his chick feed until we added a little water to it.

When our duckling wasn't sleeping,
he would get scared and "peep" loudly until
I held him, only to begin peeping again when
I would put him down. We decided to give him a
stuffed animal for companionship, a little
monkey. He snuggled next to the monkey
in his tub and stopped peeping.

As the duckling began to grow, he had a few feathers on his head that stuck straight up, which led me to name him Alfalfa. He quickly went from snuggling next to his monkey to leaning on him, resting his bill on the stuffed animal.

Alfalfa soon began to peck at or shake his
monkey with his mouth. It looked like he
was trying to kiss his new friend.

After a while, Alfalfa began to relax
and would lean on his monkey
while stretching his legs.

Before I knew it, Alfalfa
started sleeping on top of his
monkey! A duck snuggling
with a stuffed animal?
Awwww.

This photo was taken on Alfalfa's first Memorial Day, which was also his first day outside. He was scared and stayed close to his humans for most of the day.

It wasn't long before Alfalfa
began to grow fast!

He enjoys looking at his reflection
in the mirror.

Alfalfa is seen resting in the tub I first placed him in. He no longer needs the heat lamp. On this particular day, he stretched his neck all the way out and peeked over the rim of the tub! It won't be long before he outgrows the tub.

Alfalfa is too small to go into the lake without a mama duck to show him how to get himself in and out of the water, so we gave him a baby pool to splash around in.

No one had to teach him how much
fun it is to play in the water!

Alfalfa's feathers are still small and fuzzy.
As he grows bigger, a gland near his tail
will begin producing oil that he will rub all
over his feathers. Oiled feathers will not
get soaked like his current feathers.

Alfalfa seemed to wobble a bit when he walked. We realized that ducklings follow their mother ducks everywhere, which teaches them how to keep their balance. Since he thinks I'm his mama and follows me everywhere, I decided to take him on a walk through the yard each day. This will help him grow strong legs so he will be able to stand on his own.

Alfalfa is now much bigger than his monkey, but
he won't stop quacking and go to sleep if
his monkey is not near him.

I started to teach Alfalfa how to look for food in water, since he will need to know this when he's big enough to swim in the lake on his own. I started out by putting lettuce leaves or frozen corn and peas that had been thawed into his tub. He liked this!

When he's inside, Alfalfa eats pellets that are designed to keep pet ducks healthy. When he's outside, he digs for bugs in the dirt. After a rain leaves our driveway covered in worms, Alfalfa gobbles them up like he's eating spaghetti.

I love the bond that Alfalfa and I have.
There's nothing quite like it.

Alfalfa will not leave the
backyard to come to our patio
that overlooks the lake unless his
monkey comes with him. Sometimes,
I will see him pick up his monkey
in his mouth and carry him to
wherever he wants to be.
They're friends forever.

Ducks instinctively know to
keep one eye on the sky to watch
for hawks, who love to swoop down
and eat birds and other small animals.

Because Alfalfa wasn't raised in the wild, his
instincts aren't quite as sharp. After a few close
calls early on, I began placing his monkey
in areas that were out of the view of any hawks
flying overhead. Monkey isn't just a friend,
but a protector as well!

Alfalfa was about five months old before he swam in the lake by himself.
He was afraid of other ducks and geese at first, so his human family had to go in with him.
My daughter wore waders and went into the lake with him the first time. Alfalfa loved it!

Ducks find their food by putting their heads down and kicking their feet to keep their heads in the water. This is called upending or dabbling. Pekin ducks are considered "dabbling ducks." Some ducks are "diving ducks" and fully dive under water to find food to eat. When Alfalfa grabs food from the water, tiny ridges in his bill allow the water to fall out of his mouth while the food stays in his mouth.

At times, such as winter, it can be hard for the ducks to find food in the lake, so I will feed sunflower seeds to Alfalfa and the other ducks. I don't feed them bread because it's not good for them and can actually make them very sick. Sunflower seeds are nutritious and also float on the water, which makes them easier for the ducks to eat.

Alfalfa comes into the house at night, where he is safe from dangerous predators such as foxes. He is seen lying on top of his warthog, which is one of his favorite stuffed animals. He also needs his monkey close by when he sleeps. You can see it right in front of him!

Alfalfa's first winter. This was another new experience for him,
the first time he saw the lake water frozen. As he stood next to one
of his human relatives, Alfalfa stared at the lake. I wonder what
he was thinking when he didn't see water.

When the lake is frozen, I fill a tub with water for Alfalfa so he can drink and swim. Ducks need water to have clean, healthy feathers. When they take a dip in the water, they will clean bugs and dirt from each feather, spread oil onto their feathers, and make sure each feather is in it's proper place. This is called preening. Their outer feathers are waterproof and keep their feathers underneath dry. Having two layers of feathers also helps keep them warm in the winter.

A few times a year while he is molting, Alfalfa is unable to get up out of the lake so I fill his tub with water.

Birds and ducks must preen their feathers every day in order to stay healthy. For birds, this process involves cleaning their feathers with their beaks or bills, but ducks have a special oil gland near their tail that they use to keep their outer feathers waterproof, while also allowing their feathers to bend without breaking. They preen several times a day in order to stay healthy.

Ducks begin the preening process by thoroughly bathing in water,
wetting all of their feathers. This can be very exciting to watch!

After his feathers are wet, Alfalfa cranes his neck back to get oil from his oil gland, which he rubs all over his feathers using his mouth and head. This oil makes the outside of his feathers water-proof, allowing the underside of his feathers to remain dry as he swims in the lake. This is also important for ducks because it helps keep them cool in the summer and warm in the winter.

While preening, ducks can remove bugs that are stuck in their feathers so they don't get sick. They then use their mouths to realign their clean feathers. Flapping or fluffing their wings also helps put their feathers back in place. This helps make it easier for ducks to fly. Though Alfalfa and other Pekin ducks can't fly away, they are able to fly a few feet off the ground when they are in danger and must retreat to safety quickly.

Alfalfa seems to enjoy untying my sneakers,
pulling on the strings on my jackets, and tugging
on my earrings and necklaces. He is able to untie
a shoe very quickly, so if he has been standing
near my feet I have to remember to check
my shoelaces before getting up!

One summer, while making plans to go down the Jersey Shore to Cape May, we realized that all of our family members who normally stay with Alfalfa while we go out of town would be with us also. Uh-oh! We either had to stay home, or take Alfalfa with us. What's life without adventures?!

We bought an animal crate that was tall enough for Alfalfa to stand up in, gave him some pine shavings, water, and his monkey, and loaded it into the car. My husband had read that male ducks often get carsick, so I sat in the back next to Alfalfa so I could talk or sing to him to keep him calm.

Alfalfa had eaten sunflower seeds with the neighborhood ducks before we left the house, and we quickly found out that when ducks get sick they don't bend forward like most people and animals do. Instead, they shake their heads back and forth. What a surprise to see sunflower seeds shooting across the car!

From the driver's seat, my husband asked what had hit him in the back of the head and I told him, "Sunflower seeds. Alfalfa just threw up on you."

There were sunflower seeds everywhere—on the windshield, doors, and dashboard. We stopped the car and wrapped a plastic tarp around the sides of the crate for the rest of the trip, as well as for every trip to Cape May thereafter.

Once we got to the shore and took Alfalfa out of the car, he was just fine. We set up a temporary fence in the yard to keep him safe, filled a baby pool with water, and placed his monkey in the pen with him. We tried placing a beach umbrella nearby to give Alfalfa some shade, but had to put it away because it scared him and he refused to go near the umbrella or the shade it made.

Alfalfa went in and out of the pool all day long, took naps with his monkey, and got excited when people in the neighborhood (both children and adults) stopped by to see "the duck in Cape May." He loved the attention, especially from the grandchildren next door and Kelly, the neighbor in the house behind us. Alfalfa from Yardley, was a celebrity duck in Cape May!

Alfalfa has been to Cape May many times since, and the neighbors are always happy to see him. They will often stop by to visit him, bring him a stuffed animal, some fresh fruit, or sunflower seeds. Alfalfa makes friends wherever he goes.

Epilogue

In the spring of 2018, Alfalfa was about to turn six years old. We noticed that, while he was beginning to slow down a bit, he was otherwise happy and healthy. He had finally reached the point where he was comfortable exploring Lake Afton. He could often be found anywhere from one end of the lake near North Main Street to the other end, in the shallow water behind St. Andrew's playground.

On April 4, the time of year when
ducks and geese are busy building nests
and laying eggs, a Canadian goose mistakenly thought
that Alfalfa was a threat to him and his mate. I watched
as the goose attacked Alfalfa in the lake and immediately
called my husband at work.

We brought Alfalfa home and cared for him over the next
six weeks. He turned six years old on May 20 and lived
for another week before he died peacefully,
snuggled next to his monkey.

Although I am very sad that Alfalfa is gone, and I know so many people in Yardley miss him, it gives me much happiness to know that the seemingly minor decision to incubate two eggs in the spring of 2012 changed my life forever. Having the opportunity to raise Alfalfa and having him as my pet for six years turned out to be one of the best things in my life and brought me much joy. Given another opportunity to save and incubate one or more abandoned eggs at Lake Afton, I'd do it again in a heartbeat.

Published in Philadelphia, PA by Battle Ground Creative
First Edition

Battle Ground Creative is a publishing company with an emphasis on helping first-time authors find their voice. Named after an obscure city in Washington State, we currently operate offices in Houston, Texas and Philadelphia, Pennsylvania. For a complete title list and bulk order information, please visit www.battlegroundcreative.com

Edited by: Jared Stump
Cover and interior layout: Corinne Karl
All Photos © Michelle Sharer
(Except Lake Afton photo on page 42 © Jared Stump)

Softcover ISBN: 978-1-947554-93-1
Hardcover ISBN: 978-1-947554-94-8
PETS / General

Printed in the United States of America

16998144R00029

Made in the USA
Middletown, DE
03 December 2018